Cambridge Direct Mathematics

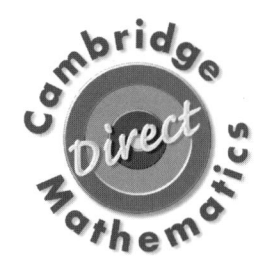

Calculations 4

Solutions

CAMBRIDGE UNIVERSITY PRESS

PUBLISHED BY THE PRESS SYNDICATE OF THE UNIVERSITY OF CAMBRIDGE
The Pitt Building, Trumpington Street, Cambridge, United Kingdom

CAMBRIDGE UNIVERSITY PRESS
The Edinburgh Building, Cambridge CB2 2RU, UK
40 West 20th Street, New York, NY 10011-4211, USA
10 Stamford Road, Oakleigh, VIC 3166, Australia
Ruiz de Alarcón 13, 28014 Madrid, Spain
Dock House, The Waterfront, Cape Town 8001, South Africa

http://www.cambridge.org

© Cambridge University Press 2000

First published 2000

Printed in the United Kingdom at the University Press, Cambridge

Typefaces Frutiger, Swift *System* QuarkXPress 4.03®

A catalogue record for this book is available from the British Library

ISBN 0 521 79826 4 paperback

General editors for Cambridge Mathematics Direct
Sandy Cowling, Jane Crowden, Andrew King, Jeanette Mumford

Writing team for *Calculations 4*
Anne Barber, Lynn Huggins-Cooper, Sandy Cowling, Zubeida Dasgupta,
Gill Hatch, Gary Murrell, Marian Reynolds, Fay Turner

The writers and publishers would like to thank the many schools and
individuals who trialled lessons for Cambridge Mathematics Direct.

NOTICE TO TEACHERS
The photocopy masters in this publication may be photocopied free of charge for
classroom use within the school or institution which purchases the publication.
Worksheets and photocopies of them remain in the copyright of Cambridge
University Press and such photocopies may not be distributed or used in any way
outside the purchasing institution. Written permission is necessary if you wish to
store the material electronically.

Notes
Solutions to textbook and copymaster questions are listed under
the title of the lesson in the teacher's handbook. Lessons are
in the same order as in the teacher's handbook.

Solutions are written in different forms:
- Complete solutions are listed wherever it is useful.
- Facsimiles of completed copymasters are included where this
  is most helpful.
- For open-ended questions and investigations, the
  possibilities are indicated through examples where this is helpful.

You can learn most about children's misconceptions by marking
their work with them or discussing incorrect answers after marking.

Solutions may be photocopied (under the conditions detailed above).

Addition and subtraction

AS1.2 Adding numbers in different orders

Pupil activities 2

10 + 10 = 20
10 + 20 = 30
10 + 30 = 40   20 + 20 = 40
10 + 40 = 50   20 + 30 = 50
10 + 50 = 60   20 + 40 = 60   30 + 30 = 60
10 + 60 = 70   20 + 50 = 70   30 + 40 = 70
10 + 70 = 80   20 + 60 = 80   30 + 50 = 80   40 + 40 = 80
10 + 80 = 90   20 + 70 = 90   30 + 60 = 90   40 + 50 = 90
10 + 90 = 100   20 + 80 = 100   30 + 70 = 100   40 + 60 = 100   50 + 50 = 100
                20 + 90 = 110   30 + 80 = 110   40 + 70 = 110   50 + 60 = 110
                                30 + 90 = 120   40 + 80 = 120   50 + 70 = 120   60 + 60 = 120
                                                40 + 90 = 130   50 + 80 = 130   60 + 70 = 130
70 + 70 = 140   50 + 90 = 140   60 + 80 = 140
70 + 80 = 150   60 + 90 = 150
70 + 90 = 160   80 + 80 = 160
                80 + 90 = 170
                                90 + 90 = 180

Solutions to □ + △ + ○ = 120:
10 + 20 + 90   10 + 30 + 80   10 + 40 + 70   10 + 50 + 60
20 + 20 + 80   20 + 30 + 70   20 + 40 + 60   20 + 50 + 50
30 + 30 + 60   30 + 40 + 50   40 + 40 + 40

AS1.3 Subtraction as taking away

TB pages 6–7

A1 a 70 − 30 = 40   b 400 − 150 = 250
    c 400 − 260 = 140   d 500 − 220 = 280
    e 80 − 40 = 40   f 1200 − 700 = 500
    g 1500 − 800 = 700

B1 a 30 − 20 = 10   b 700 − 300 = 400
    c 150 − 30 = 120   d 220 − 30 = 190

B2 a 9500 − 8300 = 1200
    b 8200 − 7600 = 600
    c 5000 − 4100 = 900
    d 6700 − 5400 = 1300

C1 a Not enough. 40 tubs were used and there are only 30 left.
    b Not enough. 250 pens were used and there are only 150 left.
    c Enough. 140 bulldog clips were used and there are 260 left.
    d Not enough. 280 erasers were used and there are only 220 left.
    e Enough. 40 red markers were used and there are 40 left.
    f Enough. 500 sticks of chalk were used and there are 700 sticks left.
    g Enough. 700 pencils were used and there are 800 left.

C2 a 6 months   b 12 months
    c 4 months   d 4 months

AS1.4 Solving problems

TB pages 8–9

★1 a 23 + 10 = 33   b 69 + 10 = 79
    c 120 + 10 = 130   d 135 + 10 = 145

★2 a 26 + 20 = 46   b 49 + 30 = 79
    c 120 + 20 = 140   d 120 + 30 = 150

A1 a 342 + 10 = 352   b 342 + 20 = 362
    c 342 + 30 = 372

A2 a 225 + 20 = 245   b 125 + 50 = 175
    c 308 + 30 = 338

A3 a 146 + 50 = 196
       They must order 5 packs.
    b 108 + 90 = 198
       They must order 9 packs (and will have 2 spare books).

c 134 + **70** = 204
   They must order 7 packs (and will have
   8 spare books).
d 103 + **100** = 203
   They must order 10 packs (and will have
   7 spare books).

B1 a 106 + **90** = 196
       They must order 9 packs.
    b 310 + **90** = 400
       They must order 9 packs (and will have
       8 spare pencils).
    c 702 + **90** = 792
       They must order 9 packs (and will have
       8 spare pens).
    d 53 + **50** = 103
       They must order 5 packs (and will have
       5 spare erasers).
    e 36 + **20** = 56
       They must order 2 packs (and will have
       7 spare pencil sharpeners).

C1 Children's own problems

Homework problem
Spending the maximum amount (90p) of change
you could buy:
9 chocolate bars; 7 chocolate bars and 1 peach;
6 chocolate bars and 1 bag of crisps;
5 chocolate bars and either 2 peaches or 1 carton
of juice;
4 chocolate bars, 1 peach and 1 bag of crisps;
3 chocolate bars and either 3 peaches or 1 peach
and 1 carton of juice or 2 bags of crisps;
2 chocolate bars, 1 bag of crisps and either 2
peaches or 1 carton of juice;
1 chocolate bar and either 2 cartons of juice or 4
peaches or 1 peach and 2 bags of crisps;
3 bags of crisps;
1 bag of crisps and either 3 peaches or 1 peach
and 1 carton of juice

AS1.5 Checking subtraction by adding

TB pages 10–11

A1 a 76p − 30p = 46p
    b 54p − 40p = 14p
    c 97p − 50p = 47p

A2 a No   45 + 30 = 75
       66 had packed lunch on Monday.
    b Yes 48 + 40 = 88
    c No   63 + 40 = 103
       53 had packed lunch on Wednesday.
    d No   39 + 40 = 79
       41 had packed lunch on Thursday.
    e Yes 44 + 50 = 94

B1 a Wrong 345 − 40 = 305
    b Wrong 793 − 60 = 733
    c Wrong 458 − 40 = 418
    d Wrong 861 − 50 = 811
    e Right

AS2.1 Explaining how to add

TB pages 12–13

A1 a 60 + 24 = 84   84p = £0.84
    b 90 + 13 = 103   103p = £1.03
    c 70 + 29 = 99   99p = £0.99
    d 80 + 34 = 114   114p = £1.14
    e 50 + 48 = 98   98p = £0.98

B1 a £1.10 + 30p = £1.40
       £1.40 + 8p = £1.48 or
       110 + 30 = 140   140 + 8 = 148
       148p = £1.48
    b £1.50 + £1 = £2.50
       £2.50 + 20p = £2.70
       £2.70 + 3p = £2.73
    c 90p + 80p = 170p
       170p + 6p = 176p = £1.76
    d £3.80 + £1 = £4.80
       £4.80 + 60p = £5.40
       £5.40 + 2p = £5.42

B2 a 250 + 312 = 562   250 + 300 = 550
       550 + 10 = 560   560 + 2 = 562
    b 399 + 580 = 979   580 + 300 = 880
       880 + 90 = 970   970 + 9 = 979
    c 1430 + 263 = 1693 1430 + 200 = 1630
       1630 + 60 = 1690   1690 + 3 = 1693
    d 580 + 401 = 981   580 + 400 = 980
       980 + 1 = 981
    e 1430 + 312 = 1742 1430 + 300 = 1730
       1730 + 10 = 1740   1740 + 2 = 1742

C1 250 + 145 = **395**
    320 + 223 = 543
    1200 + **111** = 1311
    470 + 225 = **695**
    210 + 641 = 851

C2 a £2.20 + 72p = £2.92
       Change from £5 is £2.08
    b Children's number sentences showing
       their working
    c Investigation of what can be bought
       for £10

CM 4

6 of the following:

490 + 129 = 619	490 + 47 = 537
490 + 36 = 526	490 + 387 = 877
230 + 129 = 359	230 + 47 = 277
230 + 36 = 266	230 + 387 = 617
80 + 129 = 209	80 + 47 = 127
80 + 36 = 116	80 + 387 = 467
150 + 129 = 279	150 + 47 = 197
150 + 36 = 186	150 + 387 = 537
540 + 129 = 669	540 + 47 = 587
540 + 36 = 576	540 + 387 = 927

AS2.2 Splitting numbers to add

TB pages 14–15

A1 a 43 + 24 = 60 + 7 = **67**
    b 28 + 51 = 70 + 9 = **79**
    c 123 + 46 = 100 + 60 + 9 = **169**
    d 64 + 203 = 200 + 60 + 7 = **267**

A2 a Teddy   420p
       Duck   351p
       Cowboy hat 133p
       Monkey   201p
       Frisbee   342p

    b Teddy and duck:
       420p + 351p = 771p = £7.71
       Cowboy hat and teddy:
       133p + 420p = 553p = £5.53
       Frisbee and monkey:
       342p + 201p = 543p = £5.43

B1 The only combination that cannot be bought for £10 is the teddy, the duck and the frisbee.
    For example:
    Teddy, duck and cowboy hat:
    420p + 351p + 133p = 904p = £9.04
    Teddy, monkey and frisbee:
    420p + 201p + 342p = 963p = £9.63
    Cowboy hat, monkey and frisbee:
    133p + 201p + 342p = 676p = £6.76
    Duck, monkey and frisbee:
    351p + 201p + 342p = 894p = £8.94

C1 a 411 + 324 = 735   411 + 243 = 654
       411 + 168 = 579   411 + 156 = 567
       324 + 243 = 567   324 + 168 = 492
       324 + 156 = 480   243 + 168 = 411
       243 + 156 = 399   168 + 156 = 324
    b 411 and 156, and 324 and 243 win prizes.

C2 a 411 + 324 + 243 = 978
       411 + 324 + 168 = 903
       411 + 324 + 156 = 891
       411 + 243 + 168 = 822
       411 + 243 + 156 = 810
       411 + 168 + 156 = 735
       324 + 243 + 168 = 735
       324 + 243 + 156 = 723
       324 + 168 + 156 = 648
       243 + 168 + 156 = 567
    b 243, 168 and 156 make the prize-winning total.

AS2.4 Recording addition of several numbers

TB pages 16–17

A1 a   166   b   343   c   431
      + 32   + 54   + 54
      ─────   ─────   ─────
        198   397   485

A2 a   451   b   307   c   425
      + 36   12   +164
      ─────   + 30   ─────
        487   ─────   589
                       349

    d   403   e   320
      + 96   161
      ─────   + 8
        499   ─────
                     489

B1 a   156   b   223   c   95
      + 35   + 84   +128
      ─────   ─────   ─────
        191   307   223

    d   306
      + 58
      ─────
        364

B2 Children's choices of two 3-digit numbers with the given totals, for example:

    a   361   b   132   c   713
      +120   +225   +151
      ─────   ─────   ─────
        481   357   864

C1 Children's choice of three numbers with the given totals, for example:

    a   57   b   270   c   579
         23   83   348
      + 40   + 46   + 26
      ─────   ─────   ─────
        120   399   953

(each digit 0–9 to be used once only in each part)

CM 6

1. 24 + 53 = about 70

    ```
      2 4
    + 5 3
    ─────
      7 7
    ```

2. 67 + 21 = about 90

    ```
      6 7
    + 2 1
    ─────
      8 8
    ```

3. 124 + 33 = about 150

    ```
      1 2 4
    +   3 3
    ───────
      1 5 7
    ```

4. 215 + 62 = about 280

    ```
      2 1 5
    +   6 2
    ───────
      2 7 7
    ```

AS2.5 Adding money in columns

TB pages 18–20

★1 a 137p b 302p c 99p d 298p

★2 a £1.03 b £2.31 c £3.99 d £0.32

A1 a £1.46   b £2.13   c £3.28
     + £3.11   + £1.04   + £1.37
       £4.00   £3.00   £4.00
       £0.50   £0.10   £0.50
       £0.07   £0.07   £0.15
       £4.57   £3.17   £4.65

    d £2.01   e £0.44   f £5.63
       £2.13   £1.12   £3.21
     + £1.65   + £2.03   + £1.15
       £5.79   £3.59   £9.99

A2 a £1.02   b £1.33
     + £1.29   + £1.29
       £2.31   £2.62

    c £1.02   d £1.33
       £1.67   £0.68
     + £1.29   + £1.67
       £3.98   £3.68

B1 a £439   b £215   c £439
     + £543   + £366   +£215
       £982   £581   £654

B2 a £2.26   b £4.03
     + £3.15   + £5.38
       £5.41   £9.41

    c £3.29   d £2.26
     + £3.15   £3.15
       £6.44   + £4.03
                     £9.44

C1 a £4.38   b £2.57
     + £2.25   + £4.35
       £6.00   £6.00
       £0.50   £0.80
     + £0.13   + £0.12
       £6.63   £6.92

    c £3.42   d £1.32
       £5.39   £2.29
     + £1.10   + £3.44
       £9.00   £6.00
       £0.80   £0.90
     + £0.11   + £0.15
       £9.91   £7.05

C2 a £4.49   b £3.14
       £2.15   £5.29
     + £1.36   + £1.65
       £7.00   £9.00
       £0.80   £0.90
     + £0.20   + £0.18
       £8.00   £10.08

    c £5.30   d £2.66
      £13.09   £0.07
     + £2.63   + £3.99
      £10.00   £5.00
      £10.00   £1.50
       £0.90   + £0.22
     + £0.12   £6.72
      21.02

AS3.1 Adding several small numbers

CM 7

1. 5 + 8 + 9 + 1 = 10 + 5 + 8 = 18 + 5 = 23
   Add 9 and 1, then add the largest numbers.

2. 7 + 13 + 9 = 20 + 9 = 29
   Add 7 and 13 to make 20 first.

3. 5 + 5 + 4 + 6 = 10 + 10 = 20
   Add 5 and 5 to make 10 and add 4 and 6 to make 10.

4 4 + 13 + 8 + 1 = 21 + 4 + 1 = 26
   Add the largest numbers first.

5 7 + 4 + 23 = 30 + 4 = 34
   Add 23 and 7 to make 30 first.

6 2 + □ + 7 + 9 + 1 = 36 =
   2 + □ + 7 + 10 = 2 + 17 + □ = 19 + □
   Count on from 19 to 36 to find the missing number. (17)

7 16 + □ + 4 + 6 + 6 = 43 =
   20 + □ + 12 = 32 + □
   Count on from 32 to 43 to find the missing number. (11)

8 Children's own problems

CM 8

1 Dolphins 36   Starfish 38   Whales 43
   Seahorses 36   Frogs 42
2 Whales
3 195 points altogether
4 Children's lists of strategies

AS3.2 Adding and adjusting

TB page 21

B1 a 38 + 29 = 68 − 1 = 67
    b 164 + 31 = 194 + 1 = 195
    c 73 + 59 = 133 − 1 = 132
    d 291 + 21 = 311 + 1 = 312
    e 245 + 99 = 345 − 1 = 344
    f 159 + 41 = 160 + 40 = 200

B2 With his drink, Ravi can buy:
    b (73p), c (92p), d (68p) or e (£1)

C1 With the lolly, she can buy:
    a (£1.51), b (£1.19), c (£1.38), d (£1.14),
    e (£1.46) or f (£1.68)

C2 Children's own shopping lists

CM 9

1 a 7 + 9
      is the same as 7 + 10 [17] − 1 = 16
   b 16 + 9
      is the same as 16 + 10 [26] − 1 = 25
   c 38 + 9
      is the same as 38 + 10 [48] − 1 = 47

2 a 8 + 19
      is the same as 8 + 20 [28] − 1 = 27
   b 23 + 19
      is the same as 23 + 20 [43] − 1 = 42

3 a 35 + 29
      is the same as 35 + 30 [65] − 1 = 64
   b 82 + 29
      is the same as 82 + 30 [112] − 1 = 111

4 a 68 + 11
      is the same as 68 + 10 [78] + 1 = 79
   b 43 + 21
      is the same as 43 + 20 [63] + 1 = 64
   c 76 + 31
      is the same as 76 + 30 [106] + 1 = 107

AS3.3 Subtracting and adjusting

TB pages 22–23

A1 a 67 − 19 = 47 + 1 = **48**
    b 48 − 21 = 28 − 1 = **27**
    c 53 − 31 = 23 − 1 = **22**
    d 172 − 49 = 122 + 1 = **123**

A2 a

	−39	−40	−41
76	37	36	35
92	53	52	51
58	19	18	17
84	45	44	43

    b The 3 new numbers are steps of 1 apart.
       Each is 1 smaller than the number before it.

B1 top 44p, joke book 41p, ball 38p, puzzle 29p, pen 46p

B2 top 32p, joke book 29p, ball 26p, puzzle 17p, pen 34p

C1 Children's choice of pairs with a difference of 29

C2 Children's choice of pairs with a difference of 41

C3 Children's choice of pairs with a difference of 19, 39, 49, 51 or 81

AS3.4 Add too much and take away

TB pages 24–25

A1 a 168 + 97 = 168 + 100 − 3 = **265**
    b 329 + 68 = 329 + 70 − 2 = **397**
    c 226 + 94 = 226 + 100 − 6 = **320**
    d 184 + 48 = 184 + 50 − 2 = **232**

A2 millipede 284 + 88 = 284 + 90 − 2 = 372
    ant   379 + 94 = 379 + 100 − 6 = 473
    caterpillar 83 + 19 = 83 + 20 − 1 = 102
    snail   29 + 8 = 29 + 10 − 2 = 37

B1 Totals of children's chosen pair

B2 Totals of children's 4 chosen pairs

C1 For example:
    a 284 + 29 = 284 + 30 − 1 = 313
    b 284 + 83 = 284 + 80 + 3 = 367
    c 379 + 83 = 379 + 80 + 3 = 462
    d 284 + 379 = 284 + 380 − 1 = 663

C2 Children discuss strategies.

AS3.5 Solving addition problems

TB pages 26–27

B1 a 217 + 79 = 217 + 80 − 1 = 296
    b 274 + 93 = 274 + 90 + 3 = 367
    c 144 + 108 = 144 + 110 − 2 = 252

B2 a 123 + 179 = 123 + 180 − 1 = 302
       There is enough.
    b 127 + 122 = 127 + 120 + 2 = 249
       There is not quite enough.

C1 a 45 + 109 + 46 = 91 + 109 = 200
       200 cm is enough.
    b 306 + 137 + 148
       = 300 + 6 + 140 − 3 + 150 − 2
       = 590 + 1 = 591
       200 + 200 + 100 + 100 = 600
       They need 600 cm. 591 cm is not enough.

C2 137 + 89 = 137 + 100 − 11
             = 237 − 11 = 226
    226 + 74 = 226 + 70 + 4 = 300
    They need 25 cm × 10 = 250 cm
    300 cm is enough.

C3 Children discuss strategies.

AS4.1 Halving and doubling

TB page 28

B1 a Right. Double 43 is 86
    b Wrong. Double 31 is 62
    c Right. Double 19 is 38
    d Right. Double 47 is 94
    e Right. Double 29 is 58
    f Right. Double 26 is 52
    g Right. Double 17 is 34
    h Wrong. Double 32 is 64
    i Right. Double 49 is 98
    j Wrong. Double 34 is 68

C1 Children's own doubling/halving problems based on IP 5.

CM 11

11, 22; 12, 24; 13, 26; 14, 28; 21, 42; 22, 44;
23, 46; 24, 48; 31, 62; 32, 64; 33, 66; 34, 68; 35, 70

CM 12

17, 34; 34, 68; 18, 36; 26, 52; 28, 56; 32, 64;
33, 66; 37, 74; 38, 76; 39, 78; 42, 84; 44, 88

AS4.2 Checking answers using doubles

CM 14

There are 36 possible pairs to buy:
starfish and postcard, 46p
starfish and pebbles, 47p
starfish and spade, 73p
starfish and bucket, 72p
starfish and flag, 45p
starfish and ball, 62p
starfish and sunglasses, 63p
starfish and shell, 56p
postcard and pebbles, 39p
postcard and spade, 65p
postcard and bucket, 64p
postcard and flag, 37p
postcard and ball, 54p
postcard and sunglasses, 55p
postcard and shell, 48p
pebbles and spade, 66p
pebbles and bucket, 65p
pebbles and flag, 38p
pebbles and ball, 55p
pebbles and sunglasses, 56p
pebbles and shell, 49p
spade and bucket, 91p
spade and flag, 64p
spade and ball, 81p
spade and sunglasses, 82p
spade and shell, 75p
bucket and flag, 63p
bucket and ball, 80p
bucket and sunglasses, 81p
bucket and shell, 74p
flag and ball, 53p
flag and sunglasses, 54p

flag and shell, 47p
ball and sunglasses, 71p
ball and shell, 64p
sunglasses and shell, 65p

AS4.3 Doubling 10s

TB pages 29–30

★1   a   80   b   400   c   180   d   1000

★2   a   about 280 cm   b   about 420 cm

A1   a   160   b   260   c   500   d   820
      e   720   f   380   g   700   h   940

A2   a   Cards that will fit: Hot dogs, Cola, Fizzy orange, Lemonade.
Only Cheese sandwiches will not fit.
      b   Hot dogs and Fizzy orange:
26 + 48 = 74
Check: 30 + 50 = 80   Will not fit.
Hot dogs and Cola:
26 + 18 = 44
Check: 30 + 20 = 50   Will fit.
Cola and Lemonade:
18 + 38 = 56
Check: 20 + 40 = 60   Will fit.

B1   a   440 cm   b   320 cm   c   260 cm
      d   560 cm   e   780 cm   f   1000 cm

C1   a   No. 76 + 83 = 159
Check 90 + 80 = 170
      b   There are several possible arrangements, e.g.
Bottom shelf: toy box and box of CDs
83 + 57 = 140
Check 90 + 60 = 150
Top shelf: TV, CD player and books
76 + 47 + 28 = 151
Check 80 + 50 + 30 = 160

C2   Children's designed shelf unit.

AS4.4 Using different strategies to add and subtract

TB page 31

A1   a   3 pairs from:
13 + 16 = 29   16 + 17 = 33
24 + 25 = 49   24 + 26 = 50
25 + 26 = 51   26 + 28 = 54
32 + 34 = 66   34 + 35 = 69
35 + 36 = 71   36 + 38 = 74
41 + 42 = 83   42 + 45 = 87
45 + 47 = 92
      b   3 pairs from:
16 − 13 = 3   17 − 16 = 1
25 − 24 = 1   26 − 24 = 2
26 − 25 = 1   28 − 26 = 2
34 − 32 = 2   35 − 34 = 1
36 − 35 = 1   38 − 36 = 2
42 − 41 = 1   45 − 42 = 3
47 − 45 = 2

B1   Children's own 3 pairs of numbers, added or subtracted

B2   Children's own pairs, added or subtracted

AS4.5 Choosing ways to add in columns

TB page 32

A1   You can buy any of the items singly with your £200.
You can also buy the following pairs:
watch and goggles (£197),
watch and snorkel (£200),
surf board and goggles (£147),
surf board and snorkel (£150),
surf board and flippers (£154),
surf board and oars (£167),
surf board and wet suit (£195),
dinghy and goggles (£133),
dinghy and snorkel (£136),
dinghy and flippers (£140),
dinghy and oars (£153),
dinghy and wet suit (£181),
wet suit and goggles (£84),
wet suit and snorkel (£87),
wet suit and flippers (£91),
wet suit and oars (£104),
oars and goggles (£56),
oars and snorkel (£59),
oars and flippers (£63),
flippers and goggles (£43),
flippers and snorkel (£46),
snorkel and goggles (£39)
You could also buy many groups of 3 items.

B1   a   236   b   143   c   375
        + 58   + 84   +124
         294   227   499
          1   1

d	2 6 8	e	1 8 4	f	8		
	+ 2 2 7		+ 2 7 3		1 3 9		
	4 9 5		4 5 7		+ 4 6		
	1		1		1 9 3		
					2		

B2 a £359 + £126 = £485
    b £185 + £134 = £319
    c £283 + £236 = £519
    d £236 + £179 = £415

C1 Children's suggestions for spending £750. For example a sea fishing trip for 2.

AS5.1 Using pattern to add a single digit

TB page 33

B1 Answers depend on the 4-digit numbers thrown.

C1 a 7259 + 1 = 7260   7259 + 2 = 7261
       7259 + 3 = 7262   7259 + 4 = 7263
       and 7259 + 5 = 7264
       are all less than 7262 + 3 = 7265
    b 8517 + 1 = 8518   8517 + 2 = 8519
       8517 + 3 = 8520   8517 + 4 = 8521
       8517 + 5 = 8522   8517 + 6 = 8523
       8517 + 7 = 8524   8517 + 8 = 8525
       are all less than 8521 + 5 = 8526
    Some children might also suggest fractions.

C2 186; 3, 4; 2, 6; 6, 2.

CM 15

1   2 + 5 =   7   2   8 + 5 =   13
      72 + 5 =   77   18 + 5 =   23
     472 + 5 = 477   318 + 5 = 323
    1472 + 5 = 1477   2318 + 5 = 2323

3   9 + 4 =   13   4   7 + 9 =   16
      49 + 4 =   53   27 + 9 =   36
     349 + 4 = 353   527 + 9 = 536
    4349 + 4 = 4353   6527 + 9 = 6536

5 Going clockwise round the snowflakes, from the top:
   269, 403, 452, 775, 830, 924;
   519, 934, 317, 578, 846, 385

AS5.2 Using pattern to subtract a single digit 1

TB pages 34–35

A1 a Subtract 6   b Subtract 8
       Input Output   Input Output
       500   494   500   492
       700   694   700   692
       900   894   900   892

A2 a 94p or £0.94   b 94p   c £192

B1 a Subtract 4   b Subtract 9
       Input Output   Input Output
       4000   3996   4000   3991
       7000   6996   7000   6991
       9000   8996   9000   8991

AB2 a £1.93   b £9.91   c 1993

C1 Children make up their own subtraction problems using £10.

AS5.3 Using pattern to subtract a single digit 2

TB page 36

A1 a £1.74   b £2.47   c £4.83
A2 a £6.67   b £5.56   c £123

C1 a The units digit repeats every 5 steps when you are decreasing by 2.
    b The units digit repeats every 2 steps when you are decreasing by 5.
    c The units digit repeats every 10 steps when you are decreasing by 3.
    d The units digit repeats each step when you are decreasing by 10.

C2 a 4, 8, 12, 14, 18, 22, … will also take 5 steps.
       Decreasing by 12: 100 → 88 → 76 → 64 → 52 → 40 → 28 → 16 → 4
    b 7, 13, 17, 23, … will also take 10 steps.
       Decreasing by 7: 100 → 93 → 86 → 79 → 72 → 65 → 58 → 51 → 44 → 37 → 30 → 23 →
    c 15, 25, 35, … will also take 2 steps.
       Decreasing by 15: 100 → 85 → 70 → 55 → 40 → 25 → 10

CM 18

1. −8: 2590, 2582, 2574, 2566, 2558, 2550, 2542

2. −7: 4786, 4779, 4772, 4765, 4758, 4751, 4744, 4737, 4730, 4723, 4716, 4709, 4702

3. Children's −8 and −7 sequences starting at their choice of 4-digit numbers

4. For example: When you decrease by 8, the units digit repeats after 5 steps, and when you decrease by 7, the units digit repeats after 10 steps.

AS5.4 Take too much and add back

Pupil activities

C Largest: 987 − 456 = 531
   Smallest: 745 − 698 = 47

AS5.5 Using addition and subtraction facts

TB pages 37–38

A1 a 97 − 41 = **56**   b 81 − 49 = **32**
    c 43 + 53 = **96**   d 58 + 35 = **93**

B1 a 180 + 180 = 360
    b e.g. 100 + 260 = 360
    c e.g. 99 + 261 = 360
    d e.g. 30 + 330 = 360
    e e.g. 300 + 60 = 360
    f 120 + 240 = 360

B2 b e.g. 362 − 2 = 360
    c e.g. 361 − 1 = 360
    d e.g. 370 − 10 = 360
    e e.g. 363 − 3 = 360
    f 720 − 360 = 360

C1 a 34 + **453** = 487   453 + 34 = 487
       487 − 34 = 453   487 − 453 = 34
    b **442** + 127 = 569   127 + 442 = 569
       569 − 442 = 127   569 − 127 = 442
    c 689 − **237** = 452   689 − 452 = 237
       452 + 237 = 689   237 + 452 = 689
    d 981 − **582** = 399   981 − 399 = 582
       399 + 582 = 981   582 + 399 = 981

AS6.2 ThHTU: Not much more!

Pupil activities 2

☐ − ☐ = 17 Pairs either side of 1000:
1016, 999; 1015, 998; 1014, 997; 1013, 996; 1012, 995; 1011, 994; 1010, 993; 1009, 992; 1008, 991; 1007, 990; 1006, 989; 1005, 988; 1004, 987; 1003, 986; 1002, 985; 1001, 984.

☐ − ☐ = 17 Pairs either side of 100:
116, 99; 115, 98; 114, 97; 113, 96; 112, 95; 111, 94; 110, 93; 109, 92; 108, 91; 107, 90; 106, 89; 105, 88; 104, 87; 103, 86; 102, 85; 101, 84.

☐ − ☐ = 23 Pairs either side of 4000:
4022, 3999; 4021, 3998; . . . 4001, 3978.

AS6.3 Reaching the next hundred

TB pages 39–41

A1 Answers depend on children's choice of 2-digit numbers.

A2 a 21p   b 37p   c 74p   d 42p

B1 January, 36; February, 52; March, 77; April, 63; May, 33; June, 45; July, 28; August, 19; September, 41; October, 16; November, 37; December, 77

B2 a 51p or £0.51   b 64p or £0.64
    c 81p or £0.81   d £1.15

C1 a 3600 + **400** = 4000
    b 1500 + **500** = 2000
    c 900 + **7100** = 8000
    d **9600** + 400 = 10 000

C2 Children's own questions about making up to 100 or 1000.

AS6.5 HTU − HTU: Subtraction by counting up

TB pages 42–43

★1 a £1 and 1p: £1.01   b 3p and £2: £2.03
    c 4p, 40p, £3: £3.44

A1 a   3 2 1   b   6 3 3
         − 1 6 9   − 4 7 6
         ─────────   ─────────
                 1   4
               3 0   2 0
             1 0 0   1 0 0
         +   2 1   +   3 3
         ─────────   ─────────
             1 5 2   1 5 7

A2 a   542   b   306
       − 376   − 174
       ─────   ─────
           4   6
          20   20
         100   100
       + 42   +   6
       ─────   ─────
         166   132

A3 a   £3.83   b   £8.25
       − £1.78   − £4.89
       ──────   ──────
        £0.02   £0.01
        £0.20   £0.10
        £1.00   £3.00
      + £0.83   + £0.25
       ──────   ──────
        £2.05   £3.36

B1 About £100.   £129
B2 About £1.   £1.22
B3 About £5.   £4.84
B4 About £4.   £3.90
C1 About £20.   £21.70
C2 About £4.   £4.40
C3 About £900.   £932.20

AS7.1   Starting with the units

TB pages 44–45

A1   135   A2   81
      + 47   + 138
      ─────   ─────
        182   219

A3   125
        118
      + 36
      ─────
        279

B1 423 pencils
B2 431 sheets of A3 paper
B3 455 felt pens
C1 512 notebooks
C2 1232 paperclips
C3 1212 sheets of sugar paper

AS7.2   A short way of recording in columns

TB page 46

1   a, b   There are 28 possible pairings.
2   See Plenary.

AS7.3   Carrying to other columns

TB page 47

Children should show recording in columns.

1   147 + 139 = 286
2   263 + 82 = 345
3   £6.68 + £5.26 = £11.94
4   245 + 70 = 315
5   £4.78 + £1.05 = £5.83
6   354 + 171 = 525
7   £6.35 + £3.08 = £9.43
8   253 + 229 = 482

AS7.4   Carrying across all boundaries

CM 24

    231   654   307   356
  + 524   + 32   + 565   + 38
  ─────   ─────   ─────   ─────
    755   686   872   394

    473   874   677   267
  + 462   + 43   + 248   + 555
  ─────   ─────   ─────   ─────
    935   917   925   822

AS7.5   Adding several numbers in columns

TB page 48

B1 a   123   b   £3.24
         231   £5.05
       + 45   + £0.70
       ─────   ──────
         399   £8.99

B2 a   206   b   £5.28
          73   £2.43
       + 115   + £2.05
       ─────   ──────
         394   £9.76
           1   1

B3 a   470   b   £5.45
         144   £2.54
       + 25   + £1.30
       ─────   ──────
         639   £9.29
           1   £1

B4 a   270   b   £8.10
         158   £4.74
         206   £6.18
       + 87   + £2.61
       ─────   ──────
         721   £21.63
          22   £1 1

AS8.1 Recording mental subtraction in columns

CM 25

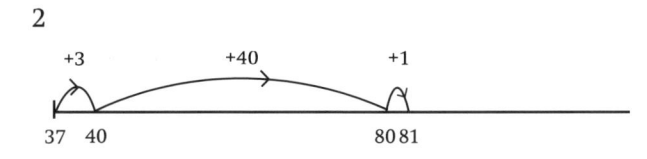

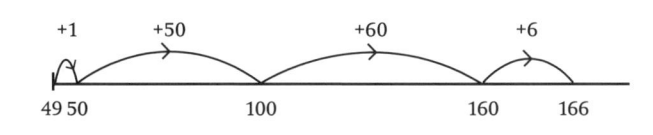

1.
```
        7 3
     -  2 6
```
add   4   to make 30
add   4 0 to make 70
add   3   to make 73
add   4 7 altogether

2.
+3, +40, +1
37 40   80 81

3.
```
       1 3 6
     -   7 8
```
add   2   to make 80
add   2 0 to make 100
add   3 0 to make 130
add   6   to make 136
add   5 8 altogether

4.
+1, +50, +60, +6
49 50   100   160 166

AS8.2 Adjusting from tens to units to help subtract

TB page 49

A1 $5^5\cancel{6}^13$ A2 $6^7\cancel{8}^15$
    $-\ \ 3\ 5$ $-\ \ 5\ 8$
    $\ \ \ 5\ 2\ 8$ $\ \ \ 6\ 2\ 7$

B1 $2^6\cancel{7}^12$ B2 $3^5\cancel{6}^15$ B3 $7^4\cancel{5}^13$
    $-\ \ \ 6\ 4$ $-\ 2\ 0\ 7$ $-\ 5\ 2\ 7$
    $\ \ \ 2\ 0\ 8$ $\ \ \ 1\ 5\ 8$ $\ \ \ 2\ 2\ 6$

C   Children's own choices of 3-digit numbers to subtract

AS8.3 Adjusting from hundreds to tens to help subtract

CM 26

1   662 = 600 + 60 + 2 = 600 + 50 + 12
    662 − 338 = 324

2   437 = 400 + 30 + 7 = 300 + 130 + 7
    437 − 83 = 354

3   254 = 200 + 50 + 4 = 100 + 150 + 4
    254 − 172 = 82

4   263 = 200 + 60 + 3 = 100 + 150 + 13
    263 − 76 = 187

5   345 = 300 + 40 + 5 = 200 + 130 + 15
    345 − 89 = 256

AS8.4 Subtracting 3-digit numbers

TB page 50

★1 a   4 5 p   b   6 6 p   c   8 2 p
       − 2 2 p   − 3 8 p   − 2 7 p
         2 3 p   2 8 p   5 5 p

★2 a   £2.35   b   £5.92   c   £4.84
       − £1.18   − £2.46   − £4.37
         £1.17   £3.46   £0.47

A1 a   1 3 6   b   2 4 2   c   3 6 0
       −   8 9   − 1 2 8   − 1 4 5
             4 7   1 1 4   2 1 5

    d   3 5 7   e   2 2 9   f   4 0 6
       − 1 8 2   − 1 7 3   − 2 8 4
           1 7 5   5 6   1 2 2

    g   3 1 4   h   2 3 1   i   3 4 1
       − 1 8 9   −   8 5   − 2 6 8
           1 2 5   1 4 6   7 3

A2 4 out of the following

     £6.50   £6.50   £6.50
   − £4.99   − £3.75   − £2.25
     £1.51   £2.75   £4.25

     £6.50   £6.50   £4.99
   − £1.25   − £0.75   − £3.75
     £5.25   £5.75   £1.24

     £4.99   £4.99   £4.99
   − £2.25   − £1.25   − £0.75
     £2.74   £3.74   £4.24

     £3.75   £3.75   £3.75
   − £2.25   − £1.25   − £0.75
     £1.50   £2.50   £3.00

     £2.25   £2.25   £1.25
   − £1.25   − £0.75   − £0.75
     £1.00   £1.50   £0.50

Multiplication and division

MD1.1   Add and multiply

TB pages 51–52

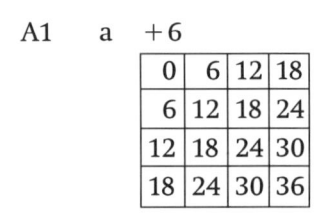

A1   a   +6

0	6	12	18
6	12	18	24
12	18	24	30
18	24	30	36

b   +8

0	8	16	24
8	16	24	32
16	24	32	40
24	32	40	48

A2   a $2 + 2 + 2 + 2 + 2 + 2 + 2 + 2$
         $= 2 \times 8 = \mathbf{16}$
     b $4 + 4 + 4 + 4 + 4 + 4 + 4$
         $= 4 \times 7 = \mathbf{28}$
     c $6 + 6 + 6 + 6 + 6 = 6 \times 5 = \mathbf{30}$
     d $8 + 8 + 8 + 8 + 8 + 8 = 8 \times 6 = \mathbf{48}$

B1   a

×	2	3	4	5
2	4	6	8	10
4	8	12	16	20
6	12	18	24	30
8	16	24	32	40

b

×	6	7	8	9
2	12	14	16	18
4	24	28	32	36
6	36	42	48	54
8	48	56	64	72

C1   a $2 \times 24 = 48$ b $4 \times 12 = 48$
     c $8 \times 6 = 48$ d $6 \times 8 = 48$

C2   a $2 \times 36 = 72$ b $4 \times 18 = 72$
     c $8 \times 9 = 72$ d $6 \times 12 = 72$

C3   Children's own totals. It is likely that they won't be able to write a multiplication sentence for each creature.

MD1.3   Multiply and divide

TB pages 53–54

A1   a $3 \times 8 = \mathbf{24}$ b $9 \times 5 = \mathbf{45}$
     c $3 \times 7 = \mathbf{21}$ d $36 \div 4 = \mathbf{9}$
     e $27 \div 3 = \mathbf{9}$ f $35 \div 5 = \mathbf{7}$

A2 $24 \div 1 = 24$ $24 \div 2 = 12$
     $24 \div 3 = 8$ $24 \div 4 = 6$
     $24 \div 6 = 4$ $24 \div 8 = 3$
     $24 \div 12 = 2$ $24 \div 24 = 1$

B1   a $28 \div 4 = 7$ b $100 \div 10 = 10$
     c $40 \div 5 = 8$

B2   a $7 \times 4 = 28$ b $10 \times 10 = 100$
     c $8 \times 5 = 40$

B3   a $6 \times 2 = 12$ $12 \div 3 = 4$ $4 \div 2 = 2$
         $2 \times 3 = 6$

     b $36 \div 4 = 9$ $9 \times 3 = 27$ $27 \div 3 = 9$
         $9 \times 4 = 36$

C1   a $18 \div 3 = 6$ $6 \times 5 = 30$ $30 \times 3 = 90$
         $90 \div 5 = 18$ or $90 \div 9 = 10$
         or $90 \div 10 = 9$ ...
     b $24 + 18 = 42$ $42 - 12 = 30$
         $30 - 18 = 12$ $12 + 12 = 24$

C2   a   The answer will always be 1.

MD2.2   Which way round?

TB page 55

★1   a $5 \times 4 = 20$
     b $4 \times 6 = 24$ $6 \times 4 = 24$
     c $7 \times 5 = 35$ $5 \times 7 = 35$
     d $3 \times 8 = 24$ $8 \times 3 = 24$
     e $6 \times 5 = 30$ $5 \times 6 = 30$
     f $4 \times 7 = 28$ $7 \times 4 = 28$

★2   Children's recording of their own arrays

A, B, C   Children's records of their own arrays

MD2.4   Using multiplication facts 1

TB pages 56–57

★1   a $4 \times 5 = \mathbf{20}$ b $3 \times 3 = \mathbf{9}$
     c $5 \times 6 = \mathbf{30}$ d $7 \times 3 = \mathbf{21}$
     e $2 \times 8 = \mathbf{16}$ f $4 \times 4 = \mathbf{16}$

★2   a $2 \times 6 = 12$ b $4 \times 6 = 24$
     c $6 \times 6 = 36$

A1   a $6 \times 4 = \mathbf{24}$ b $5 \times 8 = \mathbf{40}$
     c $3 \times 6 = \mathbf{18}$ d $5 \times 7 = \mathbf{35}$
     e $4 \times 9 = \mathbf{36}$ f $6 \times 9 = \mathbf{54}$

A2   a   8 claws and 32 legs
     b   16 claws and 64 legs
     c   14 claws and 56 legs
     d   18 claws and 72 legs

A3   For example:
     Find the number of claws and multiply by 4 to get the number of legs.
     or
     Multiply by 10 to find the total number of legs and claws. Multiply by 2 to find the number of claws. Subtract that number from the total to get the number of legs.

B1   a $6 \times 6 = \mathbf{36}$ b $6 \times 8 = \mathbf{48}$
     c $9 \times 7 = \mathbf{63}$ d $8 \times 8 = \mathbf{64}$
     e $9 \times 9 = \mathbf{81}$ f $7 \times 8 = \mathbf{56}$

B2 a $8 \times 2 \times 4 = 64$ (64 children)
    b $64 + 8 = 72$ (72 people altogether)
    c 8 balls (1 per game)
    d $3 \times 7 = 21$ (21 minutes for a game)

C1 a $9 \times 7 = 63$
    b $8 \times 8 = 64$
    c $7 \times 8 = 56$
    d $9 \times 9 = 81$ (or $3 \times 27 = 81$)
    e $7 \times 7 = 49$
    f $9 \times 6 = 54$

C2 Childrens' strategies for working out facts they did not know

C3 Children's own problems

MD3.1 Using multiplication facts 2

TB page 58

A1 a $40 \times 6 = 240$ Cost 240p or £2.40
    b $20 \times 7 = 140$ Cost 140p or £1.40
    c $50 \times 8 = 400$ Cost 400p or £4.00
    d $30 \times 9 = 270$ Cost 270p or £2.70

A2 a $(60 \times 5) + (90 \times 4) = 300 + 360 = 660$
       Cost 660p or £6.60
    b $(70 \times 6) + (80 \times 3) = 420 + 240 = 660$
       Cost 660p or £6.60

B1 a $40 \times 8 = 320$
       Change £5.00 − £3.20 = £1.80
    b $60 \times 5 = 300$
       Change £5.00 − £3.00 = £2.00
    c $90 \times 3 = 270$
       Change £5.00 − £2.70 = £2.30
    d $50 \times 7 = 350$
       Change £5.00 − £3.50 = £1.50
    e $30 \times 6 = 180$
       Change £5.00 − £1.80 = £3.20
    f $70 \times 4 = 280$
       Change £5.00 − £2.80 = £2.20

C1 a $(90 \times 4) + (40 \times 6) = 360 + 240 = 600$
       Change £10 − £6 = £4
    b $(30 \times 6) + (60 \times 4) = 180 + 240 = 420$
       Change £10.00 − £4.20 = £5.80
    c $(50 \times 5) + (30 \times 5) = 250 + 150 = 400$
       or
       $(50 + 30) \times 5 = 80 \times 5 = 400$
       Change £10.00 − £4.00 = £6.00
    d $(60 \times 8) + (20 \times 6) = 480 + 120 = 600$
       Change £10.00 − £6.00 = £4.00

CM 32

1 $3 \times 50p = 150p$
2 $6 \times 30p = 180p$
3 $8 \times 40p = 320p$
4 $9 \times 20p = 180p$
5 $(4 \times 50p) + (2 \times 40p)$
   $= 200p + 80p = 280p$
6 $(8 \times 20p) + (4 \times 30p)$
   $= 160p + 120p = 280p$
7 $(4 \times 30p) + (5 \times 40p)$
   $= 120p + 200p = 320p$
8 $(2 \times 40p) + (8 \times 20p)$
   $= 80p + 160p = 240p$

MD3.2 Multiplying with money

TB page 59

A1 a $32 \times 3 = (30 \times 3) + (2 \times 3)$
              $= 90 + 6 = 96$ Cost 96p
    b $24 \times 3 = (20 \times 3) + (4 \times 3)$
              $= 60 + 12 = 72$ Cost 72p
    c $36 \times 3 = (30 \times 3) + (6 \times 3)$
              $= 90 + 18 = 108$
       Cost 108p or £1.08
    d $28 \times 3 = (20 \times 3) + (8 \times 3)$
              $= 60 + 24 = 84$ Cost 84p
    e $17 \times 3 = (10 \times 3) + (7 \times 3)$
              $= 30 + 21 = 51$ Cost 51p
    f $43 \times 3 = (40 \times 3) + (3 \times 3)$
              $= 120 + 9 = 129$
       Cost 129p or £1.29

B1 a $32 \times 5 = (30 \times 5) + (2 \times 5)$
          $= 150 + 10 = 160$ Cost 160p or £1.60
       $24 \times 5 = (20 \times 5) + (4 \times 5)$
          $= 100 + 20 = 120$ Cost 120p or £1.20
       $36 \times 5 = (30 \times 5) + (6 \times 5)$
          $= 150 + 30 = 180$ Cost 180p or £1.80
       $28 \times 5 = (20 \times 5) + (8 \times 5)$
          $= 100 + 40 = 140$ Cost 140p or £1.40
       $17 \times 5 = (10 \times 5) + (7 \times 5)$
          $= 50 + 35 = 85$ Cost 85p or £0.85
       $43 \times 5 = (40 \times 5) + (3 \times 5)$
          $= 200 + 15 = 215$ Cost 215p or £2.15
       Total cost £9
    b Cost for 30 children is £9 × 6 = £54

C1 $36 \div 9 = 4$ So $4 \times 5 = 20$ children could come.

C2   If 30 children come, they need
     £54 − £36 = £18
     So each child needs to pay
     £18 ÷ 30 = 1800p ÷ 30 = 60p

B2   20 ÷ 3 = 6 r 2   He puts away 2 sticks.

B3   36 ÷ 5 = 7 r 1   There will be 8 piles.

B4   30 ÷ 4 = 7 r 2   8 feeding bowls are needed.

CM 33

1   3 × 25p = (3 × 20p) + (3 × 5p)
           = 60p + 15p = 75p

2   2 × 42p = (2 × 40p) + (2 × 2p)
           = 80p + 4p = 84p

3   4 × 23p = (43 × 20p) + (4 × 3p)
           = 80p + 12p = 92p

4   3 × 42p = (3 × 40p) + (3 × 2p)
           = 120p + 6p = 126p

5   4 × 28p = (4 × 20p) + (4 × 8p)
           = 80p + 32p = 112p

6   5 × 33p = (5 × 30p) + (5 × 3p)
           = 150p + 15p = 165p

CM 37

1   12 ÷ 2 = 6

2   10 ÷ 5 = 2

3   24 ÷ 4 = 6

4   18 ÷ 3 = 6

5   32 ÷ 4 = 8

6   10 ÷ 10 = 1

7   Children make up 2 sharing problems.

MD3.3   Using a grid to record TU × U (1)

CM 35

1	2 × 23 = 46	2	2 × 24 = 48
3	3 × 31 = 93	4	3 × 33 = 99
5	3 × 42 = 126	6	4 × 42 = 168
7	4 × 51 = 204	8	4 × 62 = 248
9	5 × 51 = 255	10	5 × 60 = 300

MD4.2   Rounding

TB pages 61–62

A1   24 ÷ 5 = 4 r 4
     There will be 5 plates altogether: 4 plates
     with 5 sandwiches and 1 plate with 4.

A2   10 ÷ 4 = 2 r 2
     They need 3 cars, 2 with 4 children in each,
     and one with 2 children.

A3   35 ÷ 10 = 3 r 5
     I can buy 3 bars and have 5p left over.

A4   43 ÷ 3 = 14 r 1
     14 tubes can be made. There is one ball
     left over.

A5   88 ÷ 5 = 17 r 3
     88 fish need 18 tanks, 17 tanks with 5 fish,
     and one tank with 3 fish.

B1   Children's division stories for the 3 sentences

C1   54 ÷ 7 = 7 r 5
     I need 8 trays. 7 trays with 7 cups each and
     1 more tray for the last 5 cups.

C2   75 ÷ 12 = 6 r 3
     7 minibuses. 6 full minibuses, and 1 more
     for the last 3 children.

C3   100p ÷ 9p = 11 r 1
     I can buy 11 cookies, and have 1p left over.

C4   58 ÷ 6 = 9 r 4
     58 plants will need 10 tubs.

C5   60 ÷ 8 = 7 r 4
     7 bunches of flowers can be made. There
     will be 4 flowers left over.

CM 36

Omitting the trivial answers like 68 × 1
68: 34 × 2 or 17 × 4
39: 13 × 3
85: 17 × 5
87: 29 × 3
Children's 2 numbers and multiplications

MD4.1   Sharing equally

TB page 60

A1   24 ÷ 8 = 3

A2   50 ÷ 10 = 5

A3   30 ÷ 6 = 5

A4   12 ÷ 4 = 3

B1   5 × 4 = 20 or 22 ÷ 5 = 4 r 2
     He has 2 extra apples.

C6 Children's own division sentences

MD4.3 Money problems using division

CM 38

A CD costs £6.
   It will take 12 weeks, saving 50p a week.
A can of cola costs 30p.
   10 cans can be bought for £3.
A football ticket costs £4.
   6 tickets can be bought with £25.
A book costs £2.
   It will take 10 weeks, saving 20p a week.
   It will take 5 weeks, saving 40p a week.
Chocolate bars cost 30p.
   13 bars can be bought with £4.
A computer game costs £5.
   It will take 13 weeks, saving 40p a week.
Tickets to the play cost 50p.
   £3 is only enough for 6 tickets.
A child's swimming ticket costs 40p.
   15 children can swim for £6.
Lollies cost 20p.
   40 can be bought for £8.

CM 39

A CD costs £12.
   It will take 15 weeks, saving 80p a week.
A can of cola costs 60p.
   8 cans can be bought with £5.
A football ticket costs £9.
   7 tickets can be bought with £70.
A book costs £10.
   It will take 15 weeks, saving 70p a week.
A book costs £8.
   It will take 10 weeks, saving 80p a week.
A chocolate bar costs 60p.
   15 bars can be bought for £9.
A computer game costs £10.
   It will take 17 weeks, saving 60p a week.
Tickets to the play cost £6.
   £40 is only enough for 6 tickets.
A child's swimming ticket costs 90p.
   8 children can swim for £8.
Lollies cost 70p.
   21 can be bought with £15.

MD4.4 Dividing bigger numbers

TB page 63

C1 a $150 \div 8 = 18 \text{ r } 6$
      They can fill 18 bags, and there are 6 sweets left over.
  b $95 \div 7 = 13 \text{ r } 4$
      14 plates: 13 full plates and one with 4 cakes.
  c $200 \div 9 = 22 \text{ r } 2$
      23 tables: 22 full tables and one for the last 2 children.
  d $84 \div 6 = 14$
      84 passengers will need 14 canoes.
  e $120 \div 7 = 17 \text{ r } 1$
      17 rabbits can be fed, and there is 1 carrot left over.
  f $130 \div 8 = 16 \text{ r } 2$
      You can buy 16 tickets and have £2 change.
  g $112 \div 6 = 18 \text{ r } 4$
      19 piles: 18 piles of 6 and 1 pile of 4.
  h $160 \div 9 = 17 \text{ r } 7$
      18 shelves: 17 shelves with 9 books and 1 shelf with 7.

MD5.1 Multiplying by 10 or 100

TB pages 64–65

A1 a $12 \times 10 = \mathbf{120}$ b $23 \times 10 = \mathbf{230}$
    c $35 \times 10 = \mathbf{350}$ d $5 \times 100 = \mathbf{500}$
    e $14 \times 100 = \mathbf{1400}$ f $70 \times 10 = \mathbf{700}$

A2 a $15 \times 10 = 150$ b $25 \times 10 = 250$

A3 Children's own '$\times 100$' problems

B1 a $272 \times 10 = \mathbf{2720}$ b $384 \times 10 = \mathbf{3840}$
    c $740 \times 10 = \mathbf{7400}$

B2 a $16 \times \mathbf{10} = 160$ b $51 \times \mathbf{10} = 510$
    c $\mathbf{10} \times 75 = 750$

B3 a $23 \times 100 = \mathbf{2300}$ b $48 \times 100 = \mathbf{4800}$
    c $40 \times 100 = \mathbf{4000}$ d $98 \times 100 = \mathbf{9800}$
    e $\mathbf{15} \times 100 = 1500$ f $100 \times \mathbf{10} = 1000$

B4 a $150 \times 10 = 1500$ b $25\text{p} \times 100 = £25$
    c $1250 \div 10 = 125$

C1 Children's own story problems

MD5.2 Multiplying by 'near 10' numbers

TB pages 66–67

A1 R $29 \times 9 = 29 \times 10 - 29 = 290 - 29$
               = 261 £2.61
    Y1 $30 \times 9 = 30 \times 10 - 30 = 300 - 30$
             = 270 £2.70
    Y2 $27 \times 9 = 27 \times 10 - 27 = 270 - 27$
             = 243 £2.43
    Y3 $31 \times 9 = 31 \times 10 - 31 = 310 - 31$
             = 279 £2.79
    Y4 $28 \times 9 = 28 \times 10 - 28 = 280 - 28$
             = 252 £2.52
    Y5 $32 \times 9 = 32 \times 10 - 32 = 320 - 32$
             = 288 £2.88
    Y6 $26 \times 9 = 26 \times 10 - 26 = 260 - 26$
             = 234 £2.34

A2 a $7 \times 30 = 210$ b 203

A3 $203 \times 9 = 203 \times 10 - 203 = 2030 - 203$
            = 1827 £18.27

B1 Children's calculations generated by 1–100 number cards

C1 Children's choice of 3-digit numbers to multiply by 9 and 11

MD5.3 Using a grid to record TU × U (2)

CM 35

1 $6 \times 21 = 126$ 2 $6 \times 32 = 192$
3 $7 \times 31 = 217$ 4 $7 \times 43 = 301$
5 $7 \times 52 = 364$ 6 $8 \times 31 = 248$
7 $8 \times 44 = 352$ 8 $9 \times 11 = 99$
9 $9 \times 25 = 225$ 10 $9 \times 46 = 414$

CM 42

Less than 96: $2 \times 43 = 86$ $3 \times 29 = 87$
                  $8 \times 11 = 4 \times 22 = 2 \times 44 = 88$
                  $2 \times 45 = 3 \times 30 = 6 \times 15 = 90$
                  $7 \times 13 = 91$
                  $2 \times 46 = 4 \times 23 = 92$
                  $3 \times 31 = 93$ $2 \times 47 = 94$
                  $5 \times 19 = 95$

On target: $2 \times 48 = 3 \times 32 = 4 \times 24$
                      = $6 \times 16 = 8 \times 12$

More than 96: $2 \times 49 = 7 \times 14 = 98$
                    $3 \times 33 = 9 \times 11 = 99$
                    $2 \times 50 = 4 \times 25$
                      = $5 \times 20 = 100$

$2 \times 51 = 3 \times 34 = 6 \times 17 = 102$
$2 \times 52 = 4 \times 26 = 8 \times 13 = 104$
$3 \times 35 = 5 \times 21 = 7 \times 15 = 105$

MD5.4 Solving problems with TU × U

CM 43

Seals eat 34 fish a day.
   6 seals need $34 \times 6 = 204$ fish.
Each monkey gets 9 bananas.
   22 monkeys need $22 \times 9 = 198$ bananas.
The elephants eat 42 bales a day.
   They need 42×7 bales = 294 bales a week.
There are 3 postcards in a pack.
   You need 28×3 cards = 84 cards for 28 packs.
54 animals in each of 8 enclosures is 54×8
   = 432 animals altogether.
A hot air balloon can carry 18 passengers.
   5 balloons can carry $18 \times 5 = 90$ passengers.
9 key rings at 45p each cost $9 \times 45p = 405p$
   = £4.05

MD6.1 Multiplying quickly

TB page 68

A1 a $3 \times 7 = 21$ b $4 \times 5 = 20$
    c $4 \times 4 = 16$ d $9 \times 3 = 27$
    e $5 \times 6 = 30$ e $6 \times 4 = 24$

A2 a $4 \times 10 = 40$ b $8 \times 6 = 48$
    c $8 \times 4 = 32$ d $5 \times 9 = 45$
    e $7 \times 9 = 63$ f $7 \times 8 = 56$

A3 You could make 8 different sentences based on:
    $1 \times 30 = 2 \times 15 = 3 \times 10 = 5 \times 6 = 30$

B1 a $3 \times 70 = 210$ b $40 \times 5 = 200$
    c $4 \times 40 = 160$ d $60 \times 5 = 300$
    e $8 \times 50 = 400$ f $90 \times 3 = 270$

B2 a $60 \times 10 = 600$ b $6 \times 60 = 360$
    c $8 \times 40 = 320$ d $40 \times 7 = 280$
    e $80 \times 9 = 720$
    f $70 \times 8 = 80 \times 7 = 560$

B3 You could make 20 different sentences based on:
    $1 \times 240 = 2 \times 120 = 3 \times 80 = 4 \times 60$
        = $5 \times 48 = 6 \times 40 = 8 \times 30$
        = $10 \times 24 = 12 \times 20 = 15 \times 16$

MD6.2 Using columns for TU × U

TB pages 69–70

A1 a
```
    3 2
  ×   4
  ─────
  1 2 0   30 × 4
      8   2 × 4
  ─────
  1 2 8
```
b
```
    3 1
  ×   4
  ─────
  1 2 0   30 × 4
      4   1 × 4
  ─────
  1 2 4
```

A2 a
```
    2 3
  ×   3
  ─────
    6 0   20 × 3
      9   3 × 3
  ─────
    6 9
```
b
```
    2 2
  ×   3
  ─────
    6 0   20 × 3
      6   2 × 3
  ─────
    6 6
```

A3 a
```
    4 1
  ×   4
  ─────
  1 6 0   40 × 4
      4   1 × 4
  ─────
  1 6 4
```
b
```
    4 2
  ×   4
  ─────
  1 6 0   40 × 4
      8   2 × 4
  ─────
  1 6 8
```

A4 a
```
    5 1
  ×   5
  ─────
  2 5 0   50 × 5
      5   1 × 5
  ─────
  2 5 5
```
b
```
    6 1
  ×   5
  ─────
  3 0 0   60 × 5
      5   1 × 5
  ─────
  3 0 5
```

B1 a
```
    3 3
  ×   4
  ─────
  1 2 0   30 × 4
    1 2   3 × 4
  ─────
  1 3 2
```
b
```
    3 6
  ×   4
  ─────
  1 2 0   30 × 4
    2 4   6 × 4
  ─────
  1 4 4
```

B2 a
```
    4 3
  ×   5
  ─────
  2 0 0   40 × 5
    1 5   3 × 5
  ─────
  2 1 5
```
b
```
    4 5
  ×   5
  ─────
  2 0 0   40 × 5
    2 5   5 × 5
  ─────
  2 2 5
```

B3 a
```
    4 2
  ×   6
  ─────
  2 4 0   40 × 6
    1 2   2 × 6
  ─────
  2 5 2
```
b
```
    4 4
  ×   6
  ─────
  2 4 0   40 × 6
    2 4   4 × 6
  ─────
  2 6 4
```

B4 a
```
    5 3
  ×   8
  ─────
  4 0 0   50 × 8
    2 4   3 × 8
  ─────
  4 2 4
```
b
```
    5 5
  ×   8
  ─────
  4 0 0   50 × 8
    4 0   5 × 8
  ─────
  4 4 0
```

C1   21 × 2 = 42   42 × 2 = 84
   so 21 × 4 = 84
      26 × 2 = 52   52 × 2 = 104
   so 26 × 4 = 104
      32 × 2 = 64   64 × 2 = 128
   so 32 × 4 = 128
      43 × 2 = 86   86 × 2 = 172
   so 43 × 4 = 172
      55 × 2 = 110   110 × 2 = 220
   so 55 × 4 = 220

C2   22 × 2 = 44   44 × 2 = 88
   so 22 × 6 = 132
      31 × 2 = 62   62 × 2 = 124
   so 31 × 6 = 186
      43 × 2 = 86   86 × 2 = 172
   so 43 × 6 = 258
      52 × 2 = 104   104 × 2 = 208
   so 52 × 6 = 312
      64 × 2 = 128   128 × 2 = 156
   so 64 × 6 = 284

C3 They would find 6× the number, then add on the number.

MD6.3 TU × U: tens first

TB page 71

A1 a
```
    4 4
  ×   4
  ─────
  1 6 0
    1 6
  ─────
  1 7 6
```
b
```
    5 4
  ×   4
  ─────
  2 0 0
    1 6
  ─────
  2 1 6
```
c
```
    6 4
  ×   4
  ─────
  2 4 0
    1 6
  ─────
  2 5 6
```

d
```
    3 5
  ×   4
  ─────
  1 2 0
    2 0
  ─────
  1 4 0
```
e
```
    3 6
  ×   4
  ─────
  1 2 0
    2 4
  ─────
  1 4 4
```
f
```
    3 7
  ×   4
  ─────
  1 2 0
    2 8
  ─────
  1 4 8
```

A2 a 44 × 2 = 88   88 × 2 = 176
    b 54 × 2 = 108   108 × 2 = 216
    c 64 × 2 = 128   128 × 2 = 256
    d 35 × 2 = 70   70 × 2 = 140
    e 36 × 2 = 72   72 × 2 = 144
    f 37 × 2 = 74   74 × 2 = 148

B1 a $\begin{array}{r} 55 \\ \times\ 3 \\ \hline 150 \\ 15 \\ \hline 165 \end{array}$ b $\begin{array}{r} 63 \\ \times\ 5 \\ \hline 300 \\ 15 \\ \hline 315 \end{array}$ c $\begin{array}{r} 68 \\ \times\ 3 \\ \hline 180 \\ 24 \\ \hline 204 \end{array}$

   d $\begin{array}{r} 74 \\ \times\ 5 \\ \hline 350 \\ 20 \\ \hline 370 \end{array}$ e $\begin{array}{r} 76 \\ \times\ 6 \\ \hline 420 \\ 36 \\ \hline 456 \end{array}$ f $\begin{array}{r} 83 \\ \times\ 5 \\ \hline 400 \\ 15 \\ \hline 415 \end{array}$

B2 Children's choice of different method to check, e.g. using a grid

CM 45

1 $4 \times 50 = 200$ $5 \times 40 = 200$
   $8 \times 25 = 200$

2 Find a rough answer by multiplying the nearest 10 (or 5).
   Compare with facts you know, such as $50 \times 4 = 200$ or $20 \times 10 = 200$.

CM 46

13, 17, 19, 23, 29, 37, 41, 43, 59 are prime numbers, and can only be made by multiplying the number by 1.
15, 21, 26, 33, 34, 35, 46 all have one other pair of factors in addition to 1 and the number itself.
$12 = 1 \times 12 = 2 \times 6 = 3 \times 4$
$16 = 1 \times 16 = 2 \times 8 = 4 \times 4$
$18 = 1 \times 18 = 2 \times 9 = 3 \times 6$
$24 = 1 \times 24 = 2 \times 12 = 3 \times 8 = 4 \times 6$
$36 = 1 \times 36 = 2 \times 18 = 3 \times 12 = 4 \times 9 = 6 \times 6$
$42 = 1 \times 42 = 2 \times 21 = 3 \times 14 = 6 \times 7$
$45 = 1 \times 45 = 3 \times 15 = 5 \times 9$
$48 = 1 \times 48 = 2 \times 24 = 3 \times 16 = 4 \times 12 = 6 \times 8$
$50 = 1 \times 50 = 2 \times 25 = 5 \times 10$
$52 = 1 \times 52 = 2 \times 26 = 4 \times 13$
$54 = 1 \times 54 = 2 \times 27 = 3 \times 18 = 6 \times 9$
$60 = 1 \times 60 = 2 \times 30 = 3 \times 20 = 4 \times 15$
$ = 5 \times 12 = 6 \times 10$

MD6.5 TU × U: short multiplication

TB page 73

B1 $\begin{array}{r} 27 \\ \times\ 7 \\ \hline 189 \\ 14 \end{array}$

B2 Sticks of fudge cost less than 20p so she can buy at least 5. Could she buy 6?

$\begin{array}{r} 18 \\ \times\ 6 \\ \hline 108 \\ 4 \end{array}$ 6 cost more than £1 so she can buy only 5.

B3 $\begin{array}{r} 16 \\ \times\ 9 \\ \hline 144 \\ 5 \end{array}$ Cost 144p or £1.44. Change 6p.

B4 $\begin{array}{r} 34 \\ \times\ 6 \\ \hline 204 \\ 2 \end{array}$ 6 bars cost 204p or £2.04 which is more than Jake has.

B5 Children's choices of purchases for £5

MD7.2 Dividing 2-digit numbers

TB pages 74–75

★1 a $40 \div 5 = 8$ 8 cards each
    b $44 \div 4 = 11$
    c $24 \div 3 = 8$ 8 groups
    d $30 \div 10 = 3$
    e $32 \div 5 = 6 \text{ r } 2$ 32 is not divisible by 5.
    f $36 \div 4 = 9$ 4 is a factor of 36.

A1 a $85 \div 5 = 17$
    b $88 \div 4 = 22$
    c $66 \div 3 = 22$ (22 groups)
    d $90 \div 9 = 10$
    e No. $92 \div 5 = 18 \text{ r } 2$
    f Yes. $96 \div 6 = 16$

B1 a $78 \div 6 = 13$
    b $86 \div 8 = 10 \text{ r } 6$
    c $42 \div 5 = 8 \text{ r } 2$ (8 groups)
    d Yes. $84 \div 7 = 12$
    e No. $98 \div 8 = 12 \text{ r } 2$
    f $97 \div 5 = 19 \text{ r } 2$

C1 a 60   b 60 or 96
    c 53, 59, 61, 67, 71, 73, 79, 83, 89, 97

MD7.3 Using columns to record TU ÷ U
TB pages 76–77

★1 a
```
    42
 -  30    10 × 3
 ─────
    12
 -  12    4 × 3
 ─────
     0
```
42 ÷ 3 = 10 + 4
      = 14

b
```
    56
 -  40    10 × 4
 ─────
    16
 -  16    4 × 4
 ─────
     0
```
56 ÷ 4 = 10 + 4
      = 14

★2
```
    62
 -  40    10 × 4
 ─────
    22
 -  20    5 × 4
 ─────
     2
```
a 15 fish each   b 2 left over

A1 a 14   b 15   c 17
    d 13   e 23   f 27
    g 16   h 19
The message is: VISIT THE ZOO

B1 a
```
    78
 -  60    10 × 6
 ─────
    18
 -  18    3 × 6
 ─────
     0
```
78 ÷ 6 = 13

b
```
    98
 -  80    10 × 8
 ─────
    18
 -  16    2 × 8
 ─────
     2
```
98 ÷ 8 = 12 r 2

c
```
    89
 -  70    10 × 7
 ─────
    29
 -  28    4 × 7
 ─────
     1
```
89 ÷ 7 = 14 r 1

B2 a 83 + 12 = 95   95 ÷ 4 = 23 r 3
       They need 24 tables.
    b 83 ÷ 3 = 27 r 2
       They get 28 packs.
    c 93 ÷ 6 = 15 r 3
       There are 16 groups of monkeys.

C1 a 53, 57, 61, 65, 69, 73, 77, 81, 85, 89, 93, 97
       The numbers increase in steps of 4.
    b 52, 57, 62, 67, 72, 77, 82, 87, 92, 97
       The numbers increase in steps of 5.

C2 57, 77, 97 are in both patterns. They
    increase in steps of 4 × 5 = 20

C3 a 52, 55, 58, 61, 64, 67, 70, 73, 76, 79, 82,
       85, 88, 91, 94, 97, 100
    b 55, 61, 67, 73, 79, 85, 91, 97
    The numbers in b are all included in a.

C4 Children's investigation of their own choice of numbers

MD7.4 Introducing short division
TB pages 78–79

★1 a
```
       9
  3 ) 2 7
   - 2 7   9 × 3
   ─────
       0
```
b
```
       7
  4 ) 2 8
   - 2 8   7 × 4
   ─────
       0
```
c
```
       7
  5 ) 3 5
   - 3 5   7 × 5
   ─────
       0
```

★2 a
```
       1 4
  3 ) 4 2
   - 3 0   10 × 3
   ─────
       1 2
   - 1 2   4 × 3
   ─────
       0
```
b
```
       1 4
  4 ) 5 6
   - 4 0   10 × 4
   ─────
       1 6
   - 1 6   4 × 4
   ─────
       0
```

A1 a
```
       1 2
  5 ) 6 0
   - 5 0   10 × 5
   ─────
       1 0
   - 1 0   2 × 5
   ─────
       0
```
12 packs

b
```
       1 5
  4 ) 6 0
   - 4 0   10 × 4
   ─────
       2 0
   - 2 0   5 × 4
   ─────
       0
```
15 packs

c
```
       2 0
  3 ) 6 0
   - 6 0   20 × 3
   ─────
       0
```
20 packs

A2 a
```
       1 9
  5 ) 9 5
   - 5 0   10 × 5
   ─────
       4 5
   - 4 5   9 × 5
   ─────
       0
```
19 packs

b
```
       2 3
  4 ) 9 5
   - 8 0   20 × 4
   ─────
       1 5
   - 1 2   3 × 4
   ─────
       3
```
24 packs

c
```
       3 1
  3 ) 9 5
   - 9 0   30 × 3
   ─────
       5
   - 3   1 × 3
   ─────
       2
```
32 packs

A3 Children's division stories

B1 a 12
       $8\overline{)96}$
       $\underline{-80}\quad 10\times 8$
       16
       $\underline{-16}\quad 2\times 8$
       0

   b 14
       $6\overline{)84}$
       $\underline{-60}\quad 10\times 6$
       24
       $\underline{-24}\quad 4\times 6$
       0

   c 14
       $7\overline{)98}$
       $\underline{-70}\quad 10\times 7$
       28
       $\underline{-28}\quad 4\times 7$
       0

B2 a $12\quad\text{r}\,4$
       $6\overline{)76}$
       $\underline{-60}\quad 10\times 6$
       16
       $\underline{-12}\quad 2\times 6$
       4

   b $13\quad\text{r}\,2$
       $7\overline{)93}$
       $\underline{-70}\quad 10\times 7$
       23
       $\underline{-21}\quad 3\times 7$
       2

   c $11\quad\text{r}\,6$
       $8\overline{)94}$
       $\underline{-80}\quad 10\times 8$
       14
       $\underline{-8}\quad 1\times 8$
       6

C1 a ✓ $95 \div 5 = 19$ b ✗ $79 \div 3 = 26\,\text{r}\,1$
    c ✗ $86 \div 4 = 21\,\text{r}\,2$ d ✓ $90 \div 6 = 15$
    e ✗ $94 \div 6 = 15\,\text{r}\,4$ f ✓ $96 \div 8 = 12$
    g ✗ $93 \div 3 = 31$ h ✗ $93 \div 7 = 13\,\text{r}\,2$

C2 Children's own division questions

CM 48

1:1	5		2:	3:2	
4		4:2		5:1	6:4
	7:1	7			6
8:2				9:1	
10:3	2		11:2	4	
		12:1	5		

Solving problems

SP1.2 Patterns and rules

TB pages 80–81

A1 a 23, 26, 29   b 51, 56, 61
    c 99, 91, 83   d 24, 48, 96

A2 For example:
    a Start at 8 and keep adding 3.
    b Start at 31 and keep adding 5.
    c Start at 131 and keep taking away 8.
    d Start at 3 and keep doubling.

B1 a 4, 10, 16, 22, 28, 34
    b 100, 92, 84, 76, 68, 60
    c 8000, 4000, 2000, 1000, 500, 250
    d 2, 20, 200, 2000, 20 000, 200 000

B2 Children's rules for 4 sequences

B3 Children's examples

C   Children's investigations and general statements

SP1.3 Finding solutions

TB pages 82–83

A1 a $6 \times 8 = 48$ b $20 \div 4 = 5$
    c $30 + 26 = 56$ d $101 - 5 = 96$
    e $9 \times 10 = 90$ f $56 \div 8 = 7$

A2 a   1 8 3   b 24 28 32 36
        5 9 7   30 34 38 42
        6 4 2   36 40 44 48
                             42 46 50 54

A3 Children's word stories

B1 $\rightarrow$ +5

↓	8	13	18	23	28
+1	9	14	19	24	29
	10	15	20	25	30
	11	16	21	26	31
	12	17	22	27	**32**

B2 a $32 + 53 = 85$ b $81 - 19 = 62$
    c $42 + 68 = 110$

B3 a $160 - 24 = 136$ b $26 \div 2 = 13$
    c 3×12 or 4×9 or 6×6

C   Children's number sentences and word stories

SP2.2 Explaining how to ...

TB pages 85–86

★1   a   7 + 8 = 17   b   12 + 13 = 25
     c   24 + 25 = 29   d   18 + 19 = 37
     e   26 + 27 = 53   f   32 + 33 = 65

A   Children's examples and discussion

B1   a   0 + 1 + 2 = 3   1 + 2 + 3 = 6
       2 + 3 + 4 = 9   3 + 4 + 5 = 12
       4 + 5 + 6 = 15   5 + 6 + 7 = 18
       6 + 7 + 8 = 21   7 + 8 + 9 = 24
       8 + 9 + 10 = 27   9 + 10 + 11 = 30 ...
    b   The rule is 'Start at 3. Add 3.'

B2   0 + 1 + 2 + 3 = 6
       1 + 2 + 3 + 4 = 10
       2 + 3 + 4 + 5 = 14
       3 + 4 + 5 + 6 = 18
       ...
       26 + 27 + 28 + 29 = 110
       27 + 28 + 29 + 30 = 114

C1   a   You can make all the numbers except 4, 8, 16, and 32
    b   For example:
       All odd numbers can be made as the sum of 2 consecutive numbers.
       All even numbers that are divisible by 3 can be made as the sum of 3 consecutive numbers.

SP3.1 Using + and − to solve problems

TB pages 87–88

A1   A and B: 261 + 317 = 578
      A and C: 261 + 238 = 499
      A and D: 261 + 105 = 366
      B and C: 317 + 238 = 555
      B and D: 317 + 105 = 422
      C and D: 238 + 105 = 343

A2   a   Majorca £149 − £125 = £24
    b   Tenerife £238 − £125 = £113
    c   Egypt £357 − £149 = £208
    d   Egypt £357 − £238 = £119

B1   a   217 + 261 = 478 air miles
    b   220 + 688 = 908 air miles
    c   261 + 809 = 1070 air miles

B2   a   478 − 220 = 258 air miles
    b   908 − 898 = 20 air miles
    c   1070 − 688 = 382 air miles

C1   Children's journeys using 2000 air miles

CM 52

1   France   £3 7 8   Spain   £2 4 5
               + £3 0 1   + £1 3 1
                 £6 7 9   £3 7 6

    Majorca   £2 1 1   Italy   £4 1 6
               + £1 0 5   + £2 2 2
                 £3 1 6   £6 3 8

2   For 1 adult and 1 child the most expensive is France and the cheapest Majorca.

3   France & Spain   Spain & Majorca
       £6 7 9   £3 7 6
   − £3 7 6   − £3 1 6
       £3 0 3   £6 0

    Italy & Majorca   France & Italy
       £6 3 8   £6 7 9
   − £3 1 6   − £6 3 8
       £3 2 2   £4 1

SP3.2 Choosing which way to add or subtract

TB page 89

There are plenty of possibilities. For example:

A1   a   29 + 15 = 44 or 85 − 41 = 44
    b   513 + 42 = 555 or 389 − 56 = 333
    c   426 + 573 = 999 or 587 − 143 = 444

B1   a   25 + 14 + 60 = 99
    b   742 + 90 + 56 = 888
    c   379 + 608 + 124 = 1111
    d   1096 + 8 + 7 = 1111

C1   Children investigate winning numbers.

SP3.3 Using × and ÷ to solve problems

TB pages 90–91

A1   a   24 × 3 = **72**   b   35 × 6 = **210**
    c   21 × 4 = **84**   d   64 ÷ 2 = **32**
    e   96 ÷ 6 = **16**   f   90 ÷ 3 = **30**

A2   a   21 × 5 = 105 (105 feathers)
    b   34 × 5 = 170 (170 sequins)
    c   12 × 5 = 60 (60 cm elastic)

B1   a   48 × 6 = **288**   b   34 × 7 = **238**
    c   18 × 4 = 72   d   125 ÷ **5** = 25
    e   232 ÷ 8 = **29**   f   168 ÷ 7 = **24**

B2 a 23 × 6 = 138   (138 pipecleaners)
    b 23 × 9 = 207   (207 leopard's spots)
    c 23 × 8 = 184   (184 cm elastic)

B3 Children's own mask design and workings

C1 Class 4 needs 28 × 6 = 168
    That leaves 190 − 168 = 22
    There are not enough for Class 3.

C2 Children's own problem

Assessment

CM 54

How long was it to the year 2000 when
Jamie was born in 1987   Yes
Laura scored 167 points in a word game and
Zoe scored 98.
By how many points did Laura win?   Maybe
Charlie had 102 marbles but lost 7.
How many does she have now?   No
Fay paid £5.65 for some tennis balls. David
bought the same ones for £4.95.
How much cheaper were David's?   Maybe
At Christmas St Fredrick's School had 402
children. 8 children left
How many are there in January?   No
Jessica scored 83 on her new computer game.
Her friend Tom scored 57.
By how many points did she beat him?   Maybe

(Yes, when the numbers are close; No, when a single-digit number is subtracted; Maybe, when the number to be subtracted is close to a 'hundred' or 'ten' and you can count on in 10s or 100s, which is easier than counting back.)

CM 55

1	254
	− 132
	―――
	   122
		2	£8.63
			− £2.28
			――――
			   £6.35

3	842
	− 460
	―――
	   382
		4	£7.34
			− £5.56
			――――
			   £1.78

5	£32.42 − £28.63 ――――― £3.79		